WHEN I FIRST MET THE *Prophet*

First Impressions of the Prophet Joseph Smith

WHEN I FIRST MET THE *Prophet*

First Impressions of the Prophet Joseph Smith

Compiled by
Douglas J. Vermeeren

CFI
Springville, Utah

© 2007 Douglas Vermeeren

All rights reserved.

No part of this book may be reproduced in any form whatsoever, whether by graphic, visual, electronic, film, microfilm, tape recording, or any other means, without prior written permission of the publisher, except in the case of brief passages embodied in critical reviews and articles.

This is not an official publication of The Church of Jesus Christ of Latter-day Saints. The opinions and views expressed herein belong solely to the author and do not necessarily represent the opinions or views of Cedar Fort, Inc. Permission for the use of sources is also solely the responsibility of the author. Spelling and grammar have been modernized.

ISBN 13: 978-1-59955-023-7

Published by CFI, an imprint of Cedar Fort, Inc., 2373 W. 700 S., Springville, UT, 84663
Distributed by Cedar Fort, Inc., www.cedarfort.com

LIBRARY OF CONGRESS CATALOGING-IN-PUBLICATION DATA

When I first met the prophet : first impressions of the Prophet Joseph Smith/ compiled by Douglas Vermeeren.
  p. cm.
ISBN 978-1-59955-023-7 (alk. paper)
1. Smith, Joseph, 1805-1844. I. Vermeeren, Douglas J. II. Title.

BX8695.S6W44 2007
289.3092--dc22
[B]

2007000594

Cover design by Nicole Williams
Cover design © 2007 by Lyle Mortimer

Printed in the United States of America

10 9 8 7 6 5 4 3 2 1

Printed on acid-free paper

Contents

Introduction ix
William Adams 1
Alvah Alexander 2
William Appleby 2
Millen Atwood 3
Jonah Ball 3
Israel Barlow 4
John F. Bellows 4
Gilbert Belnap 6
Ezra T. Benson 6
George David Black Jr. 8
Jane Johnston Black 8
Peter H. Burnett 9
George Q. Cannon 10
John M. Chidester 11
William Clayton 11
Zebedee Coltrin 12
Howard Coray 13
Martha Jane Knowlton Coray 14
Oliver Cowdery (Related By Luck Mack Smith) 14
Mathias Cowley 17

Robert Crookson Sr. 18
Philo Dibble 18
Olivia Pratt Driggs 19
Mary Dunn Ensign 19
Warren Foote 19
Samuel Kendall Gifford 20
Rachel Ridgeway Grant 20
Catherine Ellen Camp Greer 21
John Harper 21
William A. Hickman 22
Joseph Holbrook 22
Edwin Holden 22
Mary Isabella Hales Horne 23
Aaron Johnson 24
Joel Hills Johnson 24
Philo Johnson 25
William E. Jones 26
Grand Master Jonas (Mason From Columbus) 26
Dan Jones 27
Heber C. Kimball 28
Mary Ellen Kimball 28
Lydia Bailey Knight 29
Newell Knight 31
Mary Alice Cannon Lambert 32
Alfred B. Lambson 33
Christopher Layton 33
James Leech 34
Catherine Thomas Leishman 35
Mary Elizabeth Rollins Lightner 36
Louisa Littlefield 37
Lyman Omer Littlefield 38
John Lovell 39
Amasa Lyman 39

Wandle Mace	40
Daniel D. Mcarthur	41
William Mclellin	41
Samuel Miles	42
George Miller	43
Calvin W. Moore	44
Mary Adeline Beman Noble	45
John Oakley	45
David Osborn	46
Sarah M. Pomeroy	47
Amasa Potter	48
Orson Pratt	49
Parley P. Pratt	49
Mr. Reed	51
James Henry Rollins	52
Abraham Rose	52
Edwin Rushton (Related By His Son)	53
Bathsheba W. Smith	54
George A. Smith	55
Jesse N. Smith	55
Job F. Smith	56
Joseph F. Smith	56
Lucy Meserve Smith	57
Eliza R. Snow	58
Lorenzo Snow	59
Edward Stevenson	61
Joseph Taylor	61
William Taylor	62
James P. Terry	62
John H. Tippets	63
Daniel Tyler	63
Emmeline Blanche Wells	64
Eliza Westover	66

Joel William White	66
Elizabeth Ann Whitney	67
Helen Mar Whitney	67
Walter Wilcox	68
Mary Ann Stearns Winters	69
Catherine Haskell Woodbury	69
Wilford Woodruff	70
Mariah Woodward	71
Andrew Workman	72
Brigham Young	72

Introduction

We've all heard the saying, "You never get a second chance to make a great first impression." First impressions are lasting. Often we form our lifelong opinions about things and people within the first few seconds of interaction. First impressions are very powerful.

I have been impressed by how early members of the Church were affected when they first met the Prophet Joseph. However, it wasn't until I met a prophet of God myself that I understood more clearly some of the emotions these early Saints must have felt. It was this meeting with President Gordon B. Hinckley that prompted me to research and assemble this volume.

My own experience with President Hinckley was quite simple. But it had a very profound and lasting effect. It was an event I will always remember. It was in the late fall of 2001. Business had taken me to Salt Lake City, Utah. While there I had an extra two days, so I decided to stay. I toured the Church buildings and sites near Temple Square on Saturday and then decided to stay nearby for the Sabbath.

When I awoke the next morning, I realized I didn't know where the nearest meetinghouse was. However, I knew in Salt Lake City I wouldn't have a hard time solving that problem. So I started on foot up to Temple Square. When I got there, I was quickly informed that there was a meeting available in the Joseph Smith Memorial Building. I directed my course there and instantly found I was just slightly early for an elders quorum meeting. I joined in.

After a Sunday School meeting, we entered a large hall converted into a sacrament room. I sat down and began chatting with members around me. Suddenly everyone stood up, and I was caught a little off guard. I turned to see what the commotion was when suddenly I recognized the face of the prophet. He had entered the room with his wife.

I did not expect to see him, and I was immediately struck by a flurry of emotions. One of them was disbelief that I had so randomly chosen his home ward.

As he entered and took his seat, the sacrament program resumed as normal. It was a testimony meeting.

At the conclusion, the congregation again rose as President and Sister Hinckley left the room. Members crowded around the couple as they made their way toward an elevator. I made my way closer in the group to simply get a better look at them.

I was impressed by their kindness and smile for everyone. My focus shifted to the prophet. I was awestruck that a man at his age was so aware and considerate of all around him. He shook hands with young children, stopped to notice the babies, took the hands of the older folks, and seemed to know many by name.

I moved in a little closer. I must have caught his eye, for he then he turned toward me. He took my hand and shook it. And even though he didn't know my name, I had a distinct feeling that he was an interested friend. He was a pleasure to everyone who encountered him.

I will not easily forget that Sunday morning. I am confident that this is typical of the greeting President Hinckley leaves with everyone he meets.

I have no doubt that the Prophet Joseph Smith must have also left this same gift with all he met.

Each of these first meetings and impressions in this volume have been selected not because of their unique nature, but because they are typical of how the Prophet Joseph Smith interacted with the Saints. I believe they truly display his personality, character, and prophetic nature.

As you will notice, Joseph Smith was a genuine man and was sincerely interested in people. It is also interesting to me that although he suffered countless difficulties at the hands of his many oppressors, he had great faith and commitment to his mission and calling. He even extended a courteous hand of friendship to his enemies.

Everywhere he went he encouraged people to be better and sustained them in their challenges. This is a rare attribute.

I am thankful to him for his marvelous example and inspiration. One of my students said, "It takes a man who knows Christ to be able to show Him to others." Joseph Smith was such a man.

I want to also express my deepest gratitude to those who recorded these wonderful experiences in their journals and to their families for sharing them with us.

Without the efforts of these people, we would be missing valuable insights into the personality and character of the Prophet.

FIRST IMPRESSIONS OF THE *Prophet*

WILLIAM ADAMS

I cannot express the joy and pleasure we enjoyed in first beholding the city of Nauvoo, where we could behold the prophet of God, and we were not disappointed, for he was with his brother Hyrum, leading men of the Church and other prominent men of the city, to the number of two hundred or more, who were at the landing to receive us and make us welcome to the city of the Saints. I was very happy to behold the Prophet and the Patriarch, and to have an introduction to them, and hear their voices and shake their hands.

(William Adams, "History of William Adams, Written by Himself," January 1894, typescript copy, BYU Special Collections, Harold B. Lee Library, Provo, Utah, 8–9.)

ALVAH ALEXANDER

I came to Nauvoo in the fall of 1842. At this time I met the Prophet Joseph Smith and knew him from then till the time of his death. I was only a boy of eleven when I first knew him, but I always loved him, and no amusements or games were as interesting to me as to hear him talk.

(Alvah Alexander, "Joseph Smith, the Prophet," *Young Woman's Journal* 17, no. 12 [December 1906]:541.)

——•——

WILLIAM APPLEBY

Today for the first time, I have the pleasure of seeing Brother Joseph, the Prophet! Where is the "Old Joe Smith, the Impostor, the fanatic?" with almost every other name and epithet that could be thought of applied to him, as I have heard him represented, time and again? Answer! No whererelating to him. His age is about thirty-five years, having been born in December 1805. His deportment is calm and dignified. His manners are condescending, gentle, humane, affable, and free. He converses with the meekness of a Christian, and he [has] the spirit of a pious man. A Servant and Prophet of the Most High; no ostentation, no affectation of address, no manners but candor, veracity, humility, and all the requisites that adorn. A Seer, a Revelator, appears to govern and direct his actions—You may ask him any question you please, in a becoming manner, concerning his private history, his revelations, the dealings of the Lord towards him, His politics, faith, hope, or whatever else that is consistent or reasonable to propose, and he will answer you as becomes a gentleman, even a Saint!

(William Appleby, *Autobiography and Journal* 1848–1856, holograph, LDS Church Archives, Salt Lake City, Utah.)

——•——

MILLEN ATWOOD

Filled with the "spirit of the gathering," though not yet baptized, Millen Atwood set out for Nauvoo, April 27, 1841. He arrived there on the 21st of May, and for the first time beheld the Prophet Joseph Smith. All his former ideas regarding the venerable appearance and solemn gravity of a prophet vanished like smoke when he came in contact with the genial, jocular leader of the Latter-day Saints, witnessed his frank, open manner, and felt the spell of his kindly influence. His disappointment was delight. He felt perfectly at home with the Prophet on conversing with him, for the first time, two days after his arrival.

("Millen Atwood," in Orson F. Whitney, *History of Utah*, 4 vols. [Salt Lake City, Utah: G. Q. Cannon & Sons Co., 1904], 4:55.)

— • —

JONAH BALL

When I came to [Nauvoo] Joseph Smith and about fourteen of the principal men in the Church were gone to Springfield on business of importance. The business as you will find in the papers that I am about to send. They were gone about two weeks. The next day after they returned home I called on the Prophet Joseph Smith. I had no one to introduce me, but having a letter from the Presidency at Kirtland, Ohio, for him, with injunction to deliver it myself, by which means I found an introduction to him.

There were several persons present, and we all had a social chat. I found Joseph familiar in conversation, easy and unassuming. I found no sycophancy.

("Jonah R. Ball to Harvey Howard of Shutesbury, Massachusetts, January 1843," LDS Church Archives, Salt Lake City, Utah.)

ISRAEL BARLOW

Israel has been quoted by his son, Israel II, as having said, "If I could just see this Joseph Smith, I think I could detect if he is a prophet." Israel was to make that opportunity come about, for Israel II also said that shortly thereafter his father drove in a buggy two hundred miles and visited with the Prophet for a few days. After he talked with him two or three hours, he said he knew that he was a Prophet of God.

> (Ora Haven Barlow, *The Israel Barlow Story and Mormon Mores* [Salt Lake City, Utah: Publishers Press, 1968], 97–98. Note: Another version of this story reads: "I shall see this man and know for myself if he is a prophet" [see Ora Haven Barlow, *The Israel Barlow Story and Mormon Mores* [Salt Lake City, Utah: Publishers Press, 1968], 119.)

JOHN F. BELLOWS

In the latter part of [May 1843], in company with my father, I went to Nauvoo. The next morning after we arrived there we went down to Joseph's Mansion to have an interview with the Prophet. We found him at home. He met us at the door smiling. At the same time he put out his hand and shook hands with my father first, and then grasped my hand at the same time, inviting us to come in. I cannot describe the feelings I had when he grasped my hand. I thought he was the best and noblest man my eyes ever beheld. He led us into the sitting room, where we conversed for over an hour.

Joseph and my father did most of the talking; now and then he would ask me a few questions and paid considerable attention to me.

While we were in the Prophet's house a knock was heard at the door. Joseph opened the door, and there stood two well-dressed men with tall, black stovepipe hats on. One of the men asked if Mr. Smith was in. Joseph said, "Yes, sir, I am the man." There was silence for a moment, and then Joseph spoke up and said, "Gentlemen, I know what is in your hearts, but you do not know what is in mine; and I know who you are. You are officers from Missouri to arrest me. Wait a minute," he said, "till I get my hat and I will go with you."

He turned around and made a polite bow and said, "Brother Bellows, please excuse me; call in again."

At this Father and I followed Joseph out the door. Joseph and the officers took the lead, and Father and I went on behind until we reached the gate.

Here Joseph grasped the two men, one with each arm. This aroused my curiosity. I wanted to see the end, so I followed behind. Joseph led them to where some men were working on the Nauvoo House. He led them around, and showing them the different rooms explained to them the design of the building. Presently they went inside, out of my sight. I stayed there a short time and then returned to my stopping place. I had not been there more than thirty or forty minutes when the news was all over town that the officers from Missouri had come for Joseph and that they could not find him. How he got away from the officers I never learned.

(John F. Bellows, "Recollections of the Prophet Joseph Smith," *Juvenile Instructor* 27, no. 20 [15 October 1892]: 641–42.)

— • —

GILBERT BELNAP

I was introduced to the Prophet, whose mild and penetrating glance denoted great depth of tough and extensive forethought. While [I stood] before his penetrating gaze, he seemed to read the very recesses of my heart. A thousand thoughts passed through my mind. I had been permitted by the great author of my being to behold with my natural eyes a prophet of the living God when millions had died without that privilege, and to grasp his hand in mine was a privilege that in early days I did not expect to enjoy. I seemed to be transfigured before him. I gazed with wonder at his person and listened with delight to the sound of his voice. I had this privilege both in public and private at that time and afterward. Though, in after years, I may become cast away, the impression made upon my mind at this introduction can never be erased.

The feeling which passed over me at this time is impressed upon me as indelibly and lasting as though it were written with an iron pen upon the tablets of my heart. My very destiny seemed to be interwoven with his. I loved his company; the sound of his voice was music to my ears. His counsels were good and his acts were exemplary and worthy of imitation. His theological reasoning was of God.

(Autobiography of Gilbert Belnap, BYU Library, 30.)

—— • ——

EZRA T. BENSON

In the month of July 1840, I learned that Sidney Rigdon was going to discuss with Dr. Nelson upon the principles of Mormonism. They met in a Baptist meetinghouse and being solicited by Elder Beechias Dustin to go, and hearing that the Prophet Joseph Smith was to be there, I went. The house was crowded, but Sidney Rigdon did not come. His place was supplied by Dr. Ells; they debated about two hours; the Prophet was present. This was the first time I saw him. All the arguments that Dr. Nelson used were denunciated without proof, epithets of false prophets, etc., and while he was trying to make the people believe that Joseph was the false prophet spoken of in the scriptures, Bro. Joseph looked up and smiled very pleasantly, and I thought, too much so, to be the character Nelson said he was; the meeting was adjourned to meet in a grove east of Quincy. The Prophet appointed John Cairns to continue the debate; they met according to appointment. Dr. Nelson commenced by ridiculing to a great extent the gifts of the gospel, especially the gift of tongues, and inquired how he could know whether the people spoke by the power of God or not. He said he could speak in tongues and commenced uttering a ridiculous gibberish, and he inquired if the people could tell him in what tongues he spoke, whether French, German, etc. Elder Cairns rose and showed that such characters as Nelson were to arise as foretold by Peter, in his first epistle, third chapter and third verse. "Knowing this first, that there shall come in the last days scoffers, walking after their own lusts, and saying, Where is the promise of his coming?" And thus did he prove from scripture to my satisfaction that Dr. Nelson was one of the characters through whom the truth should be evil spoken of. Dr. Nelson made another attempt to ridicule the Mormons and their doctrines, at which time he had a fit, and had it not been for his friends, he would have fallen on the platform.

(Ezra T. Benson, "Ezra Benson Autobiography," *Instructor 80*, no. 2 [February 1945]: 56.)

GEORGE DAVID BLACK JR.

My father remembered the Prophet coming to their home when he was only four years old and asking his mother if George, his father, was at home. He was riding his large black horse. Grandmother told him no, and he started to ride away. George David said, "Mother, is that the Prophet?" He stopped his horse and said, "Yes, my little man. I am the Prophet Joseph Smith; always remember that." He never forgot, and described the Prophet to his children.

<small>(See Harriet Erminie Black Garner, "Mary Hunt Black Biographical Sketch," typescript copy, LDS Church Archives, Salt Lake City, Utah.)</small>

JANE JOHNSTON BLACK

[Jane and her family] anxiously awaited Sunday to come so they could go to church and meet the Prophet Joseph Smith. Jane didn't think she could wait many more hours to see this man who was responsible for such a dramatic change in their lives. She and her family were seated on the front row, and when the Prophet walked erectly up the aisle, Jane thanked the Heavenly Father for such a blessing as to be in his presence.

The whole room stood and Jane did, too, with tears streaming down her face. He motioned for them to be seated. When he later rose to speak, Jane knew that he was God's oracle on earth. Nothing earthly had told her, but she indeed knew. When the meeting was over Brother Brigham quickly strode to the Blacks and gathered them in his arms. They had met him in England those first early days when they had been introduced to the gospel.

Then the Prophet was there beside Brigham, and he introduced them, "Brother Joseph, let me acquaint you with my friends, the Blacks, newly arrived from Manchester, Jane, George, Mary, Will, and this is Joseph."

They had gloried in hearing the Prophet's voice and now, to hold his hand. It was warm, strong and sure.

("Biographical Sketch of William 'Young' Black and Jane Johnston Black by Geniel Robertson," typescript copy, Daughters of the Utah Pioneers, Salt Lake City, Utah.)

— • —

PETER H. BURNETT

Joseph Smith Jr. was at least six feet tall, well-formed, and weighed about one hundred and eighty pounds. His appearance was not prepossessing, and his conversational powers were but ordinary. You could tell at a glance that his education was very limited. He was an awkward but vehement speaker. In conversation he was slow and used too many words to express his ideas and would not generally go directly to a point. But, with all these drawbacks, he was much more than an ordinary man. He possessed the most indomitable perseverance, was a good judge of men, and deemed himself born to command. His views were so strange and striking and his manner was so earnest, and apparently so candid, that you could not but be interested. There was a kind, familiar look about him that pleased you. He was very curteous in discussion, readily admitting what he did not intend to controvert, and would not oppose you abruptly, but had due deference to your feelings. He had the capacity for discussing a subject in different aspects and for proposing many original views, even on ordinary matters. His illustrations were his own. He had great influence over others. As evidence of this, I will state that on Thursday, just before I left to return to Liberty, I saw him out among the crowd, conversing freely with everyone, and seeming to be perfectly at ease. In the short space of five days he had managed so to mollify his enemies that he could go unprotected among them without the slightest danger. Among the Mormons he had much greater influence than Sidney Rigdon. The latter was a man of superior education, an eloquent speaker, of fine appearance and dignified manners; but he did not possess that native intellect of Smith and lacked his determined will.

(*Recollections and Opinions of an Old Pioneer*, 66–67; Peter H. Burnett, *An Old California Pioneer* [Oakland, California: Biobooks, 1946], 40–41.)

— • —

GEORGE Q. CANNON

I was a boy when my people gathered with the Saints of God. I was very curious to know the Prophet Joseph, having heard a great deal about him. I happened to be in a large crowd of people where the Prophet was, and I selected him out of that large body of people. There were no means of recognition that I know of which would suggest him to me as the Prophet; but I recognized him as though I had always known him. I am satisfied that I had known him and been familiar with him.

There are instances which all of us doubtless have known, which have proved to us that there has been a spiritual acquaintance existing between us. We frequently say, "How familiar that person's face is to me." In this way kindred spirits are brought together. We are drawn together by this knowledge and this acquaintanceship, which, I have no doubt, was formed anterior to our birth in this state of existence.

(*Collected Discourses*, edited by Brian H. Stuy, 5 vols. [Burbank, California, and Woodland Hills, Utah: B. H. S. Publishing, 1987–92], 1:235.)

JOHN M. CHIDESTER

My first recollection of seeing the Prophet Joseph Smith was at a place about sixty or seventy miles from Kirtland, where two companies of Zion's camp met. My impression on beholding the Prophet and shaking hands with him was that I stood face to face with the greatest man on earth. I testify he was a Prophet of God.

> (John M. Chidester, "Recollections of the Prophet Joseph Smith," *Juvenile Instructor* 27, no. 5 [1 March 1892]:151.)

WILLIAM CLAYTON

We have had the privilege of conversing with Joseph Smith Jr. and we are delighted with his company. We have had a privilege of ascertaining in a great measure from whence all the evil reports have arisen and hitherto have every reason to believe him innocent.

He is *not* an idiot, but a man of sound judgment, and possessed of abundance of intelligence, and whilst you listen to his conversation you receive intelligence which expands your mind and causes your heart to rejoice.

He is very familiar and delights to instruct the poor Saints. I can converse with him just as easy as I can with you, and with regard to being willing to communicate instruction he says, "I receive it freely and I will give it freely." He is willing to answer any question I have put to him and is pleased when we ask him questions. He seems exceedingly well versed in the scriptures, and whilst conversing upon any subject such light and beauty is revealed I never saw before. If I had come from England purposely to converse with him a few days, I should have considered myself well paid for my trouble.

He is no friend to iniquity but cuts at it wherever he sees it, and it is in vain to attempt to cloke it before him. He has a great measure of the spirit of God, and by this means he is preserved from imposition. He says, "I am a man of like passions with yourselves," but truly I wish I was such a man. . . .

There are some who are not good Saints and some very good ones. Joseph says that when he is out preaching he always tells the people not to come here for examples, but to set them and to copy from the Savior, who is our pattern. It is not until corn is gathered into the barn that thrashing and sorting commences. If I were in England I would raise my voice and testify that Joseph is a man of God and a prophet, that the book of Mormon is true, and this is the work of God, which will roll forth unto the ends of the earth and gather together all the good there is in the earth.

Brethren and sisters, rejoice for the Lord is God and will deliver his Saints.

("The Historian's Corner," *BYU Studies* 18, no. 3 (spring 1978): 477.)

— • —

ZEBEDEE COLTRIN

About ten days after I was confirmed a member of the Church by Lyman Wight, I first saw the Prophet Joseph at a prayer meeting at the home of Father Morley. He was then a beardless young man.

During the meeting, the powers of darkness were made manifest in a remarkable degree, causing some to make horrid noises, and others to throw themselves violently around.

Joseph said it was a fulfillment of the scriptures where it says, "That the man of sin should be revealed."

When Lyman Wight was ordained a high priest, Joseph told him he should see the heavens opened, and after he was ordained, he stood on his feet and testified that he could see the heavens open and could see Jesus standing at the right hand of God.

Harvey Whitlock was ordained next with the same promise, but afterward he seemed paralyzed. His mouth was in the shape of an italic *O,* and his arm was stretched as if nailed to a cross. Joseph rebuked the power that had seized him, and he testified, as Lyman had done, that he saw the heavens open and Jesus standing on the right hand of the Father. This was the beginning in our day of ordinations to the office of high priest.

(Address of Zebedee Coltrin at a meeting of High Priests, Spanish Fork, Utah Feb 5, 1878. High Priests record of Spanish Fork branch, from April 29, 1866 to December 1, 1898, Church historians Library, Salt Lake City Utah; Minutes of the Salt Lake City School of the Prophets, Oct. 10–11, 1883, Church Historian's Library.)

——•——

HOWARD CORAY

On the third or fourth day of April, 1840, I set out with a few others for Nauvoo for the purpose of attending conference and to gratify a curiosity that I had to see the Prophet.

Sometime during the conference, I took occasion to visit him, in company with Joseph Wood. He introduced me to Brother Joseph with something of a flourish, telling him that I was a collegiate from Jacksonville College. This was not true and was not authorized by me. The Prophet, after looking at me a little and asking me some questions, wished to know whether it would be convenient for me to come to Nauvoo and assist, or rather clerk, for him. As this was what I desired, I engaged at once to do so; and in about two weeks thereafter, I was busily employed in his office, copying a huge pile of letters into a book, correspondence with the elders as well as other persons, that had been accumulating for some time.

(Journal of Howard Coray, BYU Library, 7; Howard Coray Folder, Church Historian's Library, Salt Lake City, Utah.)

—•—

MARTHA JANE KNOWLTON CORAY

After joining the Church, she soon became acquainted with the Prophet Joseph; she said that before he was pointed out to her as the man, she could discern something in him of such a peculiar character that she knew who he was, and from her unbounded confidence in him as the man of God, she took in common hand every discourse that she heard him preach, and has carefully preserved them. Brother George A. Smith said that she had taken more pains to preserve the sayings of the great Prophet and had accomplished more in that direction than any other woman in the Church.

("Obituaries," *Woman's Exponent* 10, no. 17 [1 February 1882]: 133.)

—•—

OLIVER COWDERY

(RELATED BY LUCK MACK SMITH)

Soon after we returned from Harmony, a man by the name of Lyman Cowdery came into the neighborhood and applied to Hyrum (as he was one of the trustees) for the district school.

A meeting of the trustees was called, and Mr. Cowdery was employed. But the following day, this Mr. Cowdery brought his brother Oliver to the trustees and requested them to receive him instead of himself, as circumstances had transpired which rendered it necessary for him to disappoint them, or which would not allow of his attending to the school himself; and he would warrant the good conduct of the school under his brother's supervision.

All parties being satisfied, Oliver commenced his school, boarding for the time being at our house. He had been in the school but a short time when he began to hear from all quarters concerning the plates, and as soon began to importune Mr. Smith upon the subject, but for a considerable length of time did not succeed in eliciting any information. At last, however, he gained my husband's confidence, so far as to obtain a sketch of the facts relative to the plates.

Shortly after receiving this information, he told Mr. Smith that he was highly delighted with what he had heard, that he had been in a deep study upon the subject all day, and that it was impressed upon his mind, that he should yet have the privilege of writing for Joseph. Furthermore, that he had determined to pay him a visit at the close of school, which he was then teaching.

On coming in the following day, he said, "The subject upon which we were yesterday conversing seems working in my very bones, and I cannot for a moment get it out of my mind; finally, I have resolved on what I will do. Samuel, I understand is going down to Pennsylvania to spend the spring with Joseph; I shall make my arrangements to be ready to accompany him thither, by the time he recovers his health; for I have made it a subject of prayer, and I firmly believe that it is the will of the Lord that I should go. If there is a work for me to do in this thing, I am determined to attend to it."

Mr. Smith told him that he supposed it was his privilege to know whether this was the case, and advised him to seek for a testimony for himself, which he did, and received the witness spoken of in the book of Doctrine and Covenants, section viii.

From this time, Oliver was so completely absorbed in the subject of the record that it seemed impossible for him to think or converse about anything else.

As the time for which we had agreed for the places was now drawing to a close, we began to make preparations to remove our family and effects to the house in which Hyrum resided. We now felt more keenly than ever the injustice of the measure which had placed a landlord over us on our own premises and who was about to eject us from them.

This I thought would be a good occasion for bringing to Oliver's mind the cause of all our present privations, as well as the misfortunes which he himself was liable to if he should turn his back upon the world and set out in the service of God.

In April, Samuel and Mr. Cowdery set out for Pennsylvania. The weather for some time previous had been very wet and disagreeable—raining, freezing, and thawing alternately, which had rendered the roads almost impassable, particularly in the middle of the day. Notwithstanding, Mr. Cowdery was not to be detained either by wind or weather, and they persevered until they arrived at Joseph's. . . .

Joseph had been so hurried with his secular affairs that he could not proceed with his spiritual concerns so fast as was necessary for the speedy completion of the work; there was also another disadvantage under which he labored; his wife had so much of her time taken up with the care of her house that she could write for him but a small portion of the time. On account of these embarrassments, Joseph called upon the Lord, three days prior to the arrival of Samuel and Oliver, to send him a scribe, according to the promise of the angel; and he was informed that the same should be forth coming in a few days. Accordingly, when Mr. Cowdery told him the business that he had come upon, Joseph was not at all surprised.

They sat down and conversed together till late. During the evening Joseph told Oliver his history, as far as was necessary for his present information, in the things which mostly concerned him. And the next morning they commenced the work of translation, in which they were soon deeply engaged.

(Lucky Mack Smith, *History of Joseph Smith by His Mother*, 138–42.)

—•—

MATHIAS COWLEY

After a day or two we found an acquaintance who was very intimate with the Prophet and thereby had an introduction to him; we spent some time in conversation on matters and things as they came along, and we found the Prophet to be, what a man bearing that title ought to be—a man of God in every respect, in word, and in deed, publicly, and privately, and was loved by every good man, woman, and child. We then felt very well satisfied after seeing the Prophet of the Most High God, Joseph Smith.

("Matthias Cowley Autobiography," LDS Church Archives, Salt Lake City, Utah.)

—•—

ROBERT CROOKSON SR.

First meeting with Joseph was "the most thrilling experience of my life"; heard Joseph preach on 2 Peter in Macedonia (Ramus); said men could get their own revelation; Joseph perceived George Miller would apostatize; plural marriage taught in Nauvoo; fights against mob; some of the Saints perceived the trip to Carthage was a trip to death; tells of Saints hearing mob threats on Joseph's life.

When the river opened up we started for Nauvoo, a distance of three hundred miles.

As we approached the landing place to our great joy we saw the Prophet Joseph Smith there to welcome his people who had come so far. We were all glad to see him and set out feet upon the promised land so to speak. It was the most thrilling experience of my life, for I know that he was a Prophet of the Lord.

("Autobiography of Robert Crookston Senior," LDS Church Archives, Salt Lake City, Utah.)

PHILO DIBBLE

I saw Joseph Smith the Prophet when he first came to Kirtland. There was a branch of the Church raised up in Kirtland before he came, and at the time he arrived a variety of false spirits were manifested, such as caused jumping, shouting, falling down, etc. Joseph said, as soon as he came, "God has sent me here, and the devil must leave here, or I will."

Those delusive spirits were not seen or heard any more at that time.

(*The Junvenile Instructor*, XXVII (1 Jan. 1892), 22.)

OLIVIA PRATT DRIGGS

At Nauvoo they were met on the docks by the Prophet Joseph, who carried little Olivia in his arms up the river bank to his home, where they all received the usual welcome and "God bless you, Brother Parley."

<small>("Olivia Pratt Driggs," *Relief Society Magazine 11*, no. 8 [August 1924]: 387. Note: Olivia Pratt Driggs is the oldest daughter of Parley P. Pratt.)</small>

MARY DUNN ENSIGN

I was born 2 Nov. 1833, in Wayne County, Michigan; removed to Nauvoo in August 1841. The first person who met us was Joseph Smith the Prophet.

He stopped and shook hands with all, even the baby.

<small>("Biography of Mary Dunn Ensign, daughter of Simeon Adams Dunn and Adaline Rawson Dunn," LDS Church Archives, Salt Lake City, Utah.)</small>

WARREN FOOTE

Father came home in the spring of 1837, intending to visit Kirtland again. I concluded to accompany him. On the 8th day of May, 1837, we started our journey. The rest of our company being somewhat anxious to see the Prophet Joseph Smith and the temple concluded to accompany father and myself to Kirtland. We hired a man to take us to that place for five dollars—a distance of twelve miles. We arrived there about noon. In the afternoon we went to the Prophet's house to see him. This is the first I saw him and shook hands with him.

We went into the temple and saw the mummies and the records which were found with them. Joseph Smith Sr. explained them to us and said the records were the writings of Abraham and Joseph, Jacob's son. Some of the writings were in black and some in red. He said that the writing in red was pertaining to the Priesthood. We were also shown the temple.

("Diary of Warren Foote," cited in Foote Genealogical History [N.p.], 7; copies in private family possession.)

———•———

SAMUEL KENDALL GIFFORD

We were finally driven into Caldwell County, where I first beheld the Prophet Joseph Smith. About the first time I saw him he had gathered the Saints around him in and around an open frame structure that was being built for a school house in Far West. After the Prophet had spoken to and encouraged the Saints, refreshments were partaken of by the whole congregation. It was truly a feast to me, as if dealt out by the Savior feeding the multitude.

(S. K. Gifford, "Recollections of the Prophet Joseph Smith," *Juvenile Instructor 28*, no. 1 [1 January 1893]: 15.)

———•———

RACHEL RIDGEWAY GRANT

The first time I saw the Prophet Joseph Smith was in New Jersey, before I joined the Church. He preached there that night, but I was prejudiced at the time. I just went to hear him mostly out of curiosity. . . .

The Baptist minister and everyone warned me about going to see them. He said if I did not stop going, I must give up my place in the Baptist church; and then I went right along. I commenced to read the *Voice of Warning* and the Book of Mormon. I read nearly all night in the Book of Mormon and felt that it was true, and then I got the spirit of gathering and went to Nauvoo.

(*Young Woman's Journal*, XVI [December 1905]: 550–551.)

CATHERINE ELLEN CAMP GREER

The first time I saw the Prophet Joseph Smith, I remember him very well, and remember going to his house. My father sent me there to take some papers that were church business. He put his hand on my head and said to me, "You are a nice little red-headed girl." I liked all but the "redheaded" part. That was the first time I ever thought of him as being a Prophet. I felt such a thrill go through me as I had never felt in my life before.

My father told me it was the inspiration of the Lord, when he put his hand on me. My father said he was a Prophet of God. He was tall and straight and a nice looking man and the most beautiful man I had ever seen.

("Anecdotes and Reminiscences of Her Life as Related by Grandma Ellen C. Greer," LDS Church Archives, Salt Lake City, Utah.)

JOHN HARPER

We remained in St. Louis until the 7th of April, when Brother Snow chartered Amorant to take us to Nauvoo, where we landed on the 12th of April, and we were met at the landing by the Prophet of the Lord and some of the Twelve Apostles and a great number of the Saints. I was then fully rewarded for all that I had passed to see with my eyes and hear with my ears a living Prophet of God and hear the sweet words of his mouth blessing us in the name of the Lord God of Israel.

("Record Made by John Harper," LDS Church Archives, Salt Lake City, Utah.)

———•———

WILLIAM A. HICKMAN

In April I saw the Prophet Joseph Smith for the first time, and had a long talk with him and liked him well.

("Sketch of the Life of William A. Hickman," LDS Church Archives, Salt Lake City, Utah, 2.)

———•———

JOSEPH HOLBROOK

In the course of a few days, Joseph the Prophet came home so that I got a chance to see him when he told me much of the work of the last days, in which I hope to ever prove of great value to me.

("Autobiography of Joseph Holbrook [1806–1846]," typescript copy, BYU Special Collections, Harold B. Lee Library, Provo, Utah, 26.)

———•———

EDWIN HOLDEN

The first time I saw Joseph Smith was in 1831, in Genesee, New York state, about twenty-five miles from the famous hill, Cumorah. On hearing that two men were there calling themselves "Mormons," I determined to see them. I rode on horseback fifteen miles from the place I was living to see them—Joseph Smith and Sidney Rigdon.

When I got to the place, I learned that they were going to hold a meeting in a barn. It was so crowded that it was with much difficulty I got inside; and by a great effort climbed up on one of the beams of the roof. There I could hear them distinctly.

(Edwin Holden, "Recollections of the Prophet Joseph Smith," *Juvenile Instructor* 27, no. 5 [1 March 1892]: 153.)

——•——

MARY ISABELLA HALES HORNE

I was baptized by Orson Hyde, and ever after that our house was open for meetings and became a home for many of the elders. In the latter part of the summer of 1837 I had the great pleasure of being introduced to, and entertaining, the beloved prophet, Joseph Smith, with Sidney Rigdon and T. B. Marsh. I said to myself, "O Lord, I thank thee for granting the desire of my girlish heart, in permitting me to associate with prophets and apostles."

On shaking hands with Joseph Smith, I received the Holy Spirit in such great abundance that I felt it thrill my whole system, from the crown of my head to the soles of my feet. I thought I had never beheld so lovely a countenance. Nobility and goodness were in every feature.

("Mary Hales Autobiography," in Kenneth Glyn Hales, comp., *Windows: A Mormon Family* (Tucson, Arizona: Skyline Printing, 1985), 30–31; see also *Woman's Exponent* 11, no. 1 [1 June 1882]: 1.)

I first met the Prophet Joseph Smith in the fall of 1837, at my home in the town of Scarborough, Canada West.

When I first shook hands with him I was thrilled through and through, and I knew that he was a Prophet of God. That testimony never left me, but is still strong within me, and has been a monitor to me, so that I can now bear a faithful testimony to the divinity of the mission of that great man of God.

("The Prophet Joseph Smith: The Testimony of Sister M. Isabella Horne," *Relief Society Magazine* 38, no. 3 [March 1951]: 158.)

—•—

AARON JOHNSON

[Aaron Johnson] was baptized on 5 April 1836 by Daniel Spencer. In the spring of 1837 he and his family migrated to Kirtland to be near the Prophet.

Upon meeting him, Aaron laid forty-five hundred dollars on the Prophet's desk and proclaimed, "There is all the wealth I possess. What shall be done with it?"

Joseph took him to the window, pointed to an eighty-acre piece of land, and said, "Take your money and buy that piece of land, build you a house and it shall be yours for an inheritance, and may the Lord bless you."

("Aaron Johnson," in Susan Easton Black, *Who's Who in the Doctrine and Covenants* [Salt Lake City, Utah: Bookcraft, 1997], 149–50.)

—•—

JOEL HILLS JOHNSON

I attended the conference held in the town of Orange in Ohio, in the month of October 1831, where I first beheld the face of the Prophet and Seer, Joseph Smith. When I was introduced to him, he laid his hands on my shoulders and said to me, "I suppose you think that I am great, green, lubberly fellow."

His expression was an exact representation of his person, being large and tall and not having a particle of beard about his face. I conversed very freely with him upon many subjects relative to his mission, and received much instruction, and was highly edified and blessed of the Lord during the conference, and returned home rejoicing.

(Dairy of Joel Hills Johnson, Brigham Young University Library. Joel Hills Johnson, *Voice from the Mountains, Being a Testimony of the Truth of the Gospel of Jesus Christ, as Revealed by the Lord to Joseph Smith Jr.* [Salt Lake City, Utah: *Juvenile Instructor*, 1881], 12–13.)

— • —

PHILO JOHNSON

[Philo Johnson] moved to Nauvoo, Hancock County, Illinois, in the year 1842. He arrived at this place on the 11th of June. This was the first time that he saw the Prophet Joseph Smith.

He shook hands with him and gave him some instructions where to go to settle and to commence his business as Hatter. He seemed to be pleased with his trade, for such a business was much needed in the city. The Prophet assisted him in getting a stock of fur and lambs' wool to make hats. He went to live in one of Hyrum Smith's houses, as an office. This was located on Kimball Street. He made hats in this house four years and supplied Joseph and Hyrum Smith with all their hats; and also Brigham Young and Heber C. Kimball and Parley P. Pratt and others of the Twelve Apostles with all their wool and fur hats.

(Untitled manuscript, 18 April 1894, LDS Church Archives, Salt Lake City, Utah.)

— • —

WILLIAM E. JONES

It would be impossible for me to describe my impressions when I first saw [him]. I knew that he was a Prophet of God before I saw him, and I felt thankful to God that I was permitted to see and hear him. On the day I was baptized I received a testimony that Joseph Smith was a true Prophet, and that the Church I had entered was of divine origin.

(William E. Jones, "Recollections of the Prophet Joseph Smith," *Juvenile Instructor* 27, no. 2 [15 January 1892]: 65–66.)

———•———

GRAND MASTER JONAS
(MASON FROM COLUMBUS)

Having recently had occasion to visit the city of Nauvoo, I cannot permit the opportunity to pass without expressing the agreeable disappointment that awaited me there. I had supposed . . . that I should witness an impoverished, ignorant and bigoted population, completely priest-ridden and tyrannized by Joseph Smith, the great Prophet of these people.

On the contrary, to my surprise, I saw a people apparently happy, prosperous, and intelligent. . . . I saw no idleness, no intemperance, no noise, no riot—all appeared to be contented, with no desire to trouble themselves with anything except their own affairs.

During my stay of three days, I became acquainted with their principle men, and more particularly with their Prophet, the celebrated "old Joe Smith." I found him hospitable, polite, well informed, and liberal. . . . Of course on the subject of religion we greatly differed, but he appeared to be quite as willing to permit me to enjoy me right of opinion, as I think we ought to let the Mormons enjoy theirs.

From all I saw and heard, I am led to believe that before many years, the city of Nauvoo will be the largest and most beautiful city of the West, provided the Mormons are unmolested in the peaceable enjoyment of their rights and privileges.

(History of the Church 4:565–66.)

— • —

DAN JONES

In the summer of 1842, I entered into an arrangement with a Mr. Moffat of Augusta, Iowa, to build a boat which we named the *Maid of Iowa*. That winter I was baptized at St. Louis.

In the spring I took a load of Saints from St. Louis to Nauvoo, where I first saw the Prophet. Patting me on the shoulder from behind, in the midst of the crowd on board, he said, "God bless this little man."

The news of my embracing Mormonism injured my influence as a steamboat captain. Mr. Moffat finally complained to Joseph of sustaining an injury by my embracing Mormonism. That touched the fibers of his noble and generous soul. When I returned to Nauvoo, Joseph informed me that the unkind conduct of Mr. Moffat had won me his friendship, and that he had concluded to buy Mr. Moffat's interest in the boat, if I would take him for a partner.

(Dan Jones, "The Martyrdom of Joseph and Hyrum Smith," written 20 January, 1855, Handwritten manuscript in the Church Historian's Library, Salt Lake City, Utah.)

— • —

HEBER C. KIMBALL

In September 1832, Brothers Brigham Young and Joseph Young and myself went to Kirtland, Ohio. We saw Brother Joseph Smith and had a glorious time, during which Brother Brigham spoke in tongues, this being the first time Joseph had heard the gift. The Prophet rose up and testified that it was from God. The gift then fell upon him, and he spoke in tongues himself.

(*Woman's Exponent*, IX [1 August 1880], 39)

He rose up and testified that the gift was from God, and then the gift fell upon him and he spoke in tongues himself.

He afterwards declared it was the pure, or Adamic, language that he spoke.

Soon after this the gift of tongues commenced in the Church at Kirtland generally.

We had a precious season and returned with a blessing in our souls.

(Orson F. Whitney, *Life of Heber C. Kimball* [Salt Lake City, Utah: Stevens and Wallis, Inc., 1945], 28–29.)

—•—

MARY ELLEN KIMBALL

I first met the Prophet in the fall of 1843, at meeting, on the Temple ground.

I believed him to be a true Prophet of God, and have never had a doubt, but feel more positive daily.

(Mary Ellen Kimball, "Recollections of the Prophet Joseph Smith," *Juvenile Instructor* 27, no. 16 [15 August 1892]: 490.)

—•—

LYDIA BAILEY KNIGHT

One day in October 1833, a wagonload of people stopped at the door of Freeman Nickerson's home. They had with them two strange men—Joseph Smith and Sidney Rigdon. Although so remote from the States, rumors of a new prophet and a "golden bible" had reached Mount Pleasant, Brunt County, Ontario, Canada, and had been wondered over and commented upon.

Freeman had been told that his parents had joined the new church, and he was rather disgusted with the news. His father was indeed full of the gospel he had embraced, and was so anxious for the eternal welfare of his sons in Canada that he hitched up his carriage, gone on a visit to Kirtland, Ohio, and prevailed upon the Prophet Joseph Smith and Sidney Rigdon to accompany him on a visit to his sons, Moses and Freeman, in Mount Pleasant.

"Well, Father," said Freeman, when told who the two strangers were, "I will welcome them for your sake. But I would just about as soon as you had brought a nest of vipers and turned them loose upon us."

Moses and Freeman were wealthy merchants and men of influence in Mount Pleasant. On the evening of the arrival, after the bustle of welcome and a warm supper were over, everyone was too tired to talk, so all retired to rest.

Next morning many were the curious glances that I cast at this strange man who dared call himself a prophet. I saw a tall, well-built form, with the carriage of an Apollo; brown hair, handsome blue eyes, which seemed to dive down into the innermost thoughts with their sharp, penetrating gaze; a striking countenance, and with manners at once majestic yet gentle, dignified yet exceedingly pleasant.

Elder Rigdon was a middle-aged man of medium height, stout and quite good-looking, but without the noble grandeur that was so distinguishing a mark of the Prophet.

The Elders were very wise. They said nothing about their views or doctrines, but waited patiently until some one should express an interest.

As evening drew near, Mr. Nickerson became anxious to hear something of the newcomer's faith.

"Oh," said he to his wife, "just let him talk; I'll silence him, if he undertakes to talk about the Bible. I guess I know as much about the scriptures as he does."

As soon as supper was over, he invited his visitors and family to go upstairs to the parlor, where he said they would have some talk. "Now, Mr. Smith," he said, "I wish you and Mr. Rigdon to speak freely. Say what you wish and tell us what you believe. We will listen."

Turning to his wife he whispered, "Now you'll see how I shall shut him up."

The Prophet commenced by relating the scenes of his early life. He told how the angel had visited him, of his finding the plates and the translation of them, and gave a short account of the matter contained in the Book of Mormon.

As the speaker continued his wonderful narrative, I was listening and watching him intently. I saw his face become white and a shining glow seemed to beam from every feature.

As his story progressed, he would often allude to passages of scripture. Then Mr. Nickerson would speak up and endeavor to confound him. But the attempt was soon acknowledged even by himself to be futile.

The Prophet bore a faithful testimony that the priesthood was again restored to the earth and that God and his Son had conferred upon him the keys of the Aaronic and Melchezidek Priesthoods.

He stated that the last dispensation had come and the words of Jesus were now in force: "Go ye into all the world and preach the gospel to every creature. He that believeth and is baptized shall be saved; but he that believeth not shall be damned."

Elder Rigdon spoke after the Prophet ceased. He related some of his early experiences, and told those present that he had received a testimony for himself of the truth of what Joseph said. "God," said Elder Rigdon, "is no respecter of persons, but will give to all that ask of Him a knowledge of the things Joseph Smith has declared unto you, whether they are true or false, of God or of man."

After both men were through speaking, many questions were asked by all present, for information. The listeners were honest-hearted people, and when truth is told to such they are constrained to accept and believe.

"And is this, then," said Mr. Nickerson, "the curious religion the newspapers tell so much about? Why, if what you have said is not good sound sense, then I don't know what sense is."

A feeling of agreeable disappointment was felt by Mr. Nickerson and family, that these strange men were so different from the various representations of them.

(Lydia Knight's History, 14–23 in Journal History, 19 Oct. 1833, Church Historian's Library, Salt Lake City, Utah.)

———•———

NEWELL KNIGHT

My father lived at Colesville, Broome County, New York. He was a sober, honest man, generally respected and beloved by his neighbors and acquaintances. The business in which he was engaged often required him to have hired help, and among the many he from time to time employed was a young man by the name of Joseph Smith Jr., to whom I was particularly attached. His noble deportment, his faithfulness and his kind address could not fail to win the esteem of those who had the pleasure of his acquaintance.

One thing I will mention, which seemed to be a peculiar characteristic with him in all his boyish sports and amusements: I never knew any one to gain advantage over him, and yet he was always kind and kept the good will of his playmates.

("Newell Knight's Journal," in scraps of Biography Faith Promoting Series, Volume 10 [Salt Lake City, 1883], 47.)

— • —

MARY ALICE CANNON LAMBERT

I first saw Joseph Smith in the spring of 1843. When the boat in which we came up the Mississippi reached the landing at Nauvoo, several of the leading brethren were there to meet the company of Saints that had come on it. Among those brethren was the Prophet Joseph Smith. I knew him the instant my eyes rested upon him, and at that moment I received my testimony that he was a prophet of God, for I never had such a feeling for mortal man as then thrilled my being. He was not pointed out to me. I knew him from all the other men; and, child that I was when my eyes rested upon Joseph Smith, I knew that I saw a prophet of God.

(Mary Alice Cannon Lambert, "Joseph Smith, the Prophet," *Young Woman's Journal 16*, no. 12 [December 1905]: 554.)

— • —

ALFRED B. LAMBSON

I went to Nauvoo to visit my uncle. I put up at the Mansion House, curious to see the Prophet, and was sitting watching for him to enter. He came in and sat down. Lorin Walker put a towel about the Prophet's shoulders and dressed his hair for him, after which he got up and came over to me, lifting me bodily out of the chair, and asked: "Young man, where are you from and where are you going?"

I told him where I hailed from and that I was bound for St. Louis to join a fur company going to Oregon, to which he said: "When you join a fur company at St. Louis to go to Oregon, I will take Nauvoo on my back and carry it across the Mississippi, and set it down in Iowa," adding, "I have use for you." The Prophet made a deep impression upon me; I felt that he was superior to any man I had ever seen. In fact, if any other man had asked me those questions, I should have very soon told him it was none of his business—but what use the Prophet could have for me I could not see.

(As quoted in *Remembering Joseph*, compiled by Mark L. McConkie, 145.)

CHRISTOPHER LAYTON

We arrived in Nauvoo from Liverpool one very cold morning, April 12, 1843. There stood our Prophet on the banks of the river to welcome us. As he heartily grasped our hands, the fervently spoken words "God bless you" sank deep into our hearts, giving us a feeling of peace such as we had never known before.

(*Autobiography of Christopher Layton* [Salt Lake City, 1911], 5.)

JAMES LEECH

After arriving in Nauvoo, we were five or six weeks looking for employment, but failed to get any. One morning I said to my brother-in-law, "Let us go and see the Prophet. I feel that he will give us something to do." He considered a short time, then consented to go.

On arriving at his house we inquired for the Prophet. We were told he was over the road. So we went over and found him in a little store selling a lady some goods. This was the first time I had had an opportunity to be near him and get a good look at him. I felt there was a superior spirit in him. He was different to anyone I had ever met before; and I said in my heart, he is truly a Prophet of the most high God.

As I was not a member of the Church, I wanted Henry to ask him for work, but he did not do so, so I had to. I said, "Mr. Smith, if you please, have you any employment you could give us both, so we can get some provisions?"

He viewed us with a cheerful countenance, and with such a feeling of kindness said, "Well, boys, what can you do?"

We told him what our employment was before we left our native land.

Said he, "Can you make a ditch?"

I replied we would do the best we could at it.

"That's right, boys," and picking up a tape line he said, "Come along with me."

He took us a few rods from the store, gave me the ring to hold, and stretched all the tape from the reel and marked a line for us to work by.

"Now, boys," said he, "can you make a ditch three feet wide and two and a half feet deep along this line?

We said we would do our best, and he left us. We went to work, and when it was finished I went and told him it was done.

He came and looked at it and said, "Boys, if I had done it myself it could not have been done better. Now come with me."

He led the way back to his store, and told us to pick the best ham or piece of pork for ourselves.

Being rather bashful, I said we would rather he would give us some. So he picked two of the largest and best pieces of meat and a sack of flour for each of us, and asked us if that would do.

We told him we would be willing to do more work for it, but he said, "If you are satisfied, boys, I am."

We thanked him kindly, and went on our way home rejoicing in the kind-heartedness of the Prophet of our God.

(James Leech, "Recollections of the Prophet Joseph Smith," *Juvenile Instructor* 27, no. 5 (1 March 1892): 152–53.)

— • —

CATHERINE THOMAS LEISHMAN

We all ate breakfast at the landing, but Father said he would fast until he had seen the Prophet Joseph, to whose place he started. When within two blocks of the house the Prophet, seeing Father, crossed the street and gave his hand saying, "How are you, brother?" Father said, "I do not know you." The Prophet then said, "I am the man you are looking for," all the time holding father's hand. Father then put a piece of gold in the Prophet's hand.

Joseph said, "God bless you, brother. You shall never want for bread." He never did. The Prophet then said, "Bring your family down to my house," but Father, thanking him, said that owing to our long journey I must first get a place where we can set ourselves in order.

Then the Prophet told him he had an empty house which father rented at once. We remained at the Prophet's house until we bought a home of our own, near where the Prophet lived. All of these things were a strong testimony to my father which lasted him until his death in September 1867, aged 87 years.

("Catherine Thomas Leishman, Autobiographical Sketch," LDS Church Archives, Salt Lake City, Utah.)

———•———

MARY ELIZABETH ROLLINS LIGHTNER

John Whitmer brought a Book of Mormon to Kirtland. There was a meeting that evening, and we learned that Brother Morley had the book in his possession—the only one in that part of the country. I went to his house before the meeting and asked to see the book.

As I looked at it, I felt such a desire to read it that I could not refrain from asking him to let me take it home while he attended meeting. He finally said, "Child, if you will bring this book home before breakfast tomorrow morning you may take it."

My uncle and aunt were Methodists, so when I got into the house, I exclaimed, "Oh, Uncle, I have got the 'Golden Bible.'"

We took turns reading it until late at night.

As soon as it was light enough to see, I was up and learned the first verse in the book. When I reached Brother Morley's house, he remarked, "I guess you did not read much in it."

I showed him how far we had read.

He was surprised, and said, "I don't believe you can tell me one word of it."

I then repeated the first verse, also the outline of the history of Nephi.

He gazed at me in surprise and said, "Child, take this book home and finish it. I can wait."

About the time I finished the last chapter, the Prophet Joseph Smith arrived in Kirtland. Brother Whitney brought the Prophet Joseph to our house and introduced him to the older ones of the family. He saw the Book of Mormon on the shelf and asked how that book came to be there. He said, "I sent that book to Brother Morley."

Uncle told him how his niece had obtained it.

He asked, "Where is your niece?"

I was sent for. When he saw me, he looked at me so earnestly I felt almost afraid, and I thought, "He can read my every thought." I thought how blue his eyes were. After a moment or two, he came and put his hands on my head and gave me a great blessing, the first I ever received, and made me a present of the book, and said he would give Brother Morley another.

(Diary of Mary Elizabeth Rollins Lightner, *Young Woman's Journal*, XVI [December, 1905]: 556–57.)

LOUISA LITTLEFIELD

In Kirtland, when the wagon loads of grown people and children came in from the country meeting, Joseph would make his way to as many of the wagons as he well could and cordially shake the hand of every person. Every child and young babe in the company were especially noticed by him and tenderly taken by the hand, with his kind words and blessings. He loved innocence and purity, and he seemed to find it in the greatest perfection with the prattling child.

(*Juvenile Instructor* 27 [1 January 1892]: 24.)

LYMAN OMER LITTLEFIELD

I was a mere boy, between thirteen and fourteen years old, when I first met the Prophet. His appearance as a man won my reverence for him; but his conversation and public teaching—all attended by a power truly Godlike—established me in the faith and knowledge of his prophetic mission which strengthened with the lapse of years until he sealed his testimony with his blood in the jail at Carthage, in 1844.

(Lyman O. Littlefield, "Recollections of the Prophet Joseph Smith," *Juvenile Instructor* 27, no. 2 [15 January 1892]: 64–65.)

I first beheld him a tall, well-proportioned man, busily mingling with the members of Zion's Camp, shaking hands with them, meeting them with friendly greetings and carefully seeing to their comforts. His familiar yet courteous and dignified manner, his pleasant and intelligent countenance, his intellectual and well-formed forehead, the expressive and philanthropic facial lineaments, the pleasant smile and the happy light that beamed from his mild blue eyes; all these were among the attractive attributes that at once awakened a responsive interest in the mind of every kindly beholder, which increased in intensity as the acquaintance continued. With his most familiar friends he was social, conversational, and often indulged in harmless jokes; but when discoursing upon complicated topics that pertained to the welfare of individuals or the progressiveness of communities, his elucidations were clear and so full of common sense and genuine philosophy that the candid and fair-minded felt interested by his views, though they might decline to entertain or promulgate all of the self-evident truths he originated. Such is a brief though imperfect pen picture of this celebrated man; he was all this when I first beheld him in this traveling camp, and is it any wonder that I, so young in years, should be filled with sensations of intense pleasure and respect for him when I first met him.

(Lyman O. Littlefield, "The Prophet Joseph Smith in Zion's Camp," *Juvenile Instructor* 27, no. 1 [1 January 1892]: 56–57.)

JOHN LOVELL

John went to see the Prophet at Mr. Lawrence's home. When he first saw the Prophet, he was telling how he obtained his horse in Kirtland, Ohio. The other brethren were washing and blacking their shoes. In his journal, John says: "I had been brought up so strict to the religion of the day that I thought it impossible for a Prophet to talk about horse trades on Sunday. But their preaching overbalanced any bad effects this may have made."

("History of John Lovell," Mormon Biography File, LDS Church Archives, Salt Lake City, Utah, 3.)

AMASA LYMAN

After resting and refreshing myself for one week, I engaged to labor for Father Johnson at ten dollars per month; under this engagement I labored until the 1st of July, about which time the Prophet returned to Father Johnson's to reside. This afforded me an opportunity to see the man of God.

Of the impressions produced I will here say, although there was nothing strange or different from other men in his personal appearance, yet, when he grasped my hand in that cordial way (known to those who have met him in the honest simplicity of truth), I felt as one of old in the presence of the Lord, my strength seemed to be gone, so that it required an effort on my part to stand on my feet; but in all this there was no fear, but the serenity and peace of heaven pervaded my soul, and the still small voice of the spirit whispered its living testimony in the depths of my soul, where it has ever remained, that he was the Man of God.

("Amasa Lyman's History," *Millennial Star* 27, no. 30 [29 July 1865]: 473.)

—•—

WANDLE MACE

My eyes rested upon the great Prophet of the last days for the first time in 1839. I was introduced to him and his brother, and shook hands with them. Their sister—the wife of brother McClary—hurried to and fro, pressing them to partake of refreshments, at the same time telling them how anxious they had been, and how fearful they were lest the mob would take their lives. Joseph said to her, "You were much troubled about us, but you did not know the promises of God to us."

On landing at the top of some stairs at the back of the house the Prophet addressed the people. This is the first time I ever heard him preach, and I shall never forget his words. In the course of his remarks he said, "Yes, your name shall go out for good and evil."

(Journal of Wandle Mace, BYU Library, 36–37.)

—•—

DANIEL D. MCARTHUR

To me, he seemed to possess more power and force of character than any ordinary man. I would look upon him when he was with hundreds of other men, and he would appear greater than ever. The more I heard his sayings and saw his doings, the more I became convinced that he had of a truth seen God the Father and His Son Jesus Christ, and also the holy angels of God. If I know anything on this earth, I surely know that he was a prophet.

When Joseph Smith first spoke to me, I was in the woods about a half a mile south of Kirtland. He was on his horse and I was chopping wood. Said he, "Good afternoon."

I returned the compliment. He had a smile on his face, and I felt that he was going to say something else.

"You are not the young man who sold his wife for a bull-eye watch the other day, are you?" he asked.

I replied, "No, sir."

He went on laughing. There was a man who had sold his wife for a bull-eye watch a day or two before, and there was quite a talk about it in the neighborhood, so I supposed he thought he would have a little fun with me.

("Recollections of the Prophet Joseph Smith," *Juvenile Instructor* 27, no. 4 [15 February 1892]: 128–29.)

———•———

WILLIAM MCLELLIN

I reached Kirtland [from Independence] on the 18th day of October, and on the 25th, I attended a general conference in the town of Orange, about twenty miles distant. Here I first met and formed an acquaintance with Joseph Smith Jr., Oliver Cowdery, Sidney Rigdon, John Whitmer, etc. About 40 ministers attended the conference.

During its sittings, I, with nine others, was pointed out again by the spirit of revelation, as having the gifts and callings to the office of high priest, and was ordained thereunto under the hands of Pres. Oliver Cowdery.

Following this conference I went home with the Prophet, and on Saturday, the 29th, I received through him, and wrote from his mouth a revelation concerning myself [D&C 66]. I had expected and believed that when I saw Brother Joseph [Smith], I should receive one: and I went before the Lord in secret, and on my knees asked him to reveal the answer to five questions through his Prophet, and that too without his having any knowledge of my having made such request. I now testify in the fear of God, that every question which I had thus lodged in the ears of the Lord of Sabbath, were answered to my full and entire satisfaction. I desired it for a testimony of Joseph's inspiration. And I to this day consider it to me an evidence which I cannot refute.

(William McLellin, *Ensign of Liberty of the Church of Christ*, [Kirtland, Ohio: (s.n.), 1847–1849], 1:61.)

— • —

SAMUEL MILES

I first saw him in the town of Freedom, Catturagus County, New York, where my parents joined the Church in the early part of 1834. His kind manner and gentle words when I first met him in company with my father, and he took me by the hand; his noble deportment when before the people; his easy, jovial appearance when engaged in the sports which were common in the days of Nauvoo; his firm dislike of that which was degrading—all these combined to give me a very favorable opinion of this noble man.

(*Juvenile Instructor*, XXVII [15 March 1892]: 173.)

GEORGE MILLER

George recorded the first time he saw the Prophet: "A large man sitting in front [in a wagon] driving seemed to be familiar to me as if I had always known him, and suddenly the thought burst on my mind that it was none other than the prophet, Joseph Smith. Indeed, my whole frame was in a tremor with the occurrence of the thought." George urged the Prophet to agree to preach at a later date, but Joseph was reluctant at first because he had just escaped from prison and felt like "a bird uncaged"—he wanted to spend time with his family and friends. When he finally consented, "a time and place was fixed upon" and George "went to notify the people of the appointment of the Mormon Prophet to preach."

("George Miller," in Susan Easton Black, *Who's Who in the Doctrine and Covenants* [Salt Lake City, Utah: Bookcraft, 1997], 195–96.)

As I was in the habit of riding out every fair day, on a bland, bright morning I prevailed on my wife to indulge in the luxury of a ride on horseback to visit our tenants on the farm. On our return home, as we were leisurely riding along, I perceived a carriage containing a number of persons meeting us, and as we neared it, the appearance of a large man, sitting in front driving, seemed familiar to me, as if I had always known him, and suddenly the thought burst into my mind that it was none other than the Prophet Joseph Smith. Indeed my whole frame was in a tremor at the thought, and my heart seemed as if it were coming up into my mouth. Getting in speaking distance, he suddenly reined up his horses, as if making ready to speak. I was much agitated as the words came from his mouth. "Sir, can you tell me the way to the farm of a Mr. Miller, living somewhere in the direction I am going?"

Instead of answering him directly, my reply was, "I presume, sir, that you are Joseph Smith Jr., the Mormon Prophet." "I am, sir," he replied, adding, "I also presume that you are the Mr. Miller whose farm I inquired for." "I am, sir." He then introduced me to his wife and family, and thus a formal (or rather informal) introduction passed between us and our families.

In our short interview certain things were said in regard to our belief, that on our approach we each thought that the other was an old acquaintance. I solicited him to preach. He excused himself, not feeling able to sermonize. He said that, having just escaped from prison, he felt like a bird escaped from a cage, and was ore disposed to reconnoiter the county and visit his people and friends. Upon my urging the matter of his preaching, he suddenly turned to me, saying that he *did* think of several of the elders preaching for me, but that he was now resolved on doing it himself; that it had been whispered that a Samaritan had passed by and bound up the wounds of his bleeding friends, adding that he would do the best he could in the way of preaching. Accordingly the time and place were fixed upon, and I went to notify the people of the appointment of the Mormon Prophet to preach.

(H. W. Mills, "De Tal Palo Tal Astilla," *Annual Publications—The Historical Society of Southern California 10* [1917]: 115–16.)

— • —

CALVIN W. MOORE

When I was a small boy, my impression of him was that he was a great man and a prophet of God, and when I grew up and became older, I got a testimony for myself, and I can say that I know he was a Prophet of the living God.

(*The Juvenile Instructor*, XXVII [15 April 1892]: 255.)

MARY ADELINE BEMAN NOBLE

The next season I taught school in the neighborhood of my father. This was 1833, in the fall and winter of the same year. I commenced keeping company with Mr. Noble, and in a year, the spring of 1834, Brother Joseph Smith came from Kirtland, Ohio, to my father's New York estate, Avon, Livingston County. This was the first time I ever beheld a prophet of the Lord, and I can truly say at the first sight that I had a testimony within my bosom that he was a man chosen of God to bring forth a great work in the last days.

His society I prized. His conversation was meat and drink to me.

The principles that he brought forth bind the testimony that he bore of the truth of the Book of Mormon and made a lasting impression upon my mind.

While he was there, Sidney Rigdon and Joseph and Brigham Young, Luke and Lyman Johnson, and twelve or fourteen of the traveling elders had a council to my father's. I, in company with my sisters, had the pleasure of cooking and serving the table and waiting on them, which I considered a privilege and blessing.

("A Journal of Mary A. Noble," in "Joseph Bates Noble Autobiography," BYU Special Collections, Harold B. Lee Library, Provo, Utah, 18–19.)

JOHN OAKLEY

In the fall of 1842 I moved to Nauvoo in company with a young man by the name of Spencer. H. D. Bayless, James

Dorland, Thomas Dollinger, and their families journeyed by way of Philadelphia, Pittsburgh, Cincinatti, Louisville, [and] St. Louis. When we arrived at Nauvoo Brother Joseph Smith invited us to the upper room of the public store. He shook hands with us and informed us that his enemies had been hunting him. He greeted us warmly and told us that we must not look for perfection in him. If we did he would look for perfection in us.

(John Oakley Journal, LDS Church Archives, Salt Lake City, Utah.)

—•—

DAVID OSBORN

The first time I saw Joseph Smith was at Far West, in 1837. He and others were seated on a wagon box. There was a large congregation.

Joseph said, "You have heard many reports about me. Some perhaps are true and others not true. I know what I have done, and I know what I have not done. You may hug up to yourselves the Bible, but, except through faith in it you get revelation for yourself, the Bible will profit you but little. The Book of Mormon is true, just what it purports to be, and for this testimony I expect to give an account in the day of judgment. If I obtain the glory which I have in view, I expect to wade through much tribulation."

In his closing remarks, he said, "The Savior declared the time was coming when secret or hidden things should be revealed upon the house tops. Well, I have revealed to you a few things, if not on the house top, on the wagon top."

(*The Juvenile Instructor*, XXVII [15 March 1892], 173; Diary of David Osborn, BYU Library, 13.)

—•—

SARAH M. POMEROY

My father moved from New York to Nauvoo in the spring of 1843. I was then in my ninth year. The day after our arrival I was out in the yard when a gentleman rode up and inquired for my father, Thomas Colborn. Of course I did not know who it was, but there was something so noble and dignified in his appearance that it struck me forcibly. My father soon came out and cordially shook him by the hand and called him Brother Joseph. I knew then it was the Prophet.

It was quite an exciting time just then. The Prophet had been falsely accused of an attempt to murder Governor Boggs of Missouri. Porter Rockwell, a firm friend of Joseph, had been kidnapped and taken to Missouri as an accomplice, and was about to have his trial. Joseph requested my father to lend him a hundred dollars to pay the lawyer who defended Porter Rockwell, and Father freely counted the money.

"This shall be returned within three days, if I am alive," said the Prophet, and departed.

My aunt, Father's sister, was quite wrathful. "Don't you know, Thomas," said she, "you will never see a cent of that money again. Here are your family without a home, and you throw your money away."

"Don't worry, Katie," Father replied. "If he cannot pay it, he is welcome to it."

This conversation was held before us children, and I thought seriously about it. Would he pay it, or would he not? But I had strong faith that he would.

The day came when it was to be paid—a cold, wet, rainy day. The day passed. Night came—nine o'clock, ten o'clock—and we all retired for the night. Shortly thereafter there was a knock at the door. Father arose and went to it, and there in the driving rain stood the Prophet Joseph.

"Here, Brother Thomas, is the money." A light was struck, and he counted out the hundred dollars in gold.

He said, "Brother Thomas, I have been trying all day to raise this sum, for my honor was at stake. God bless you."

My aunt had nothing to say.

(*Young Woman's Journal*, XVII [December 1906], 538–39.)

———•———

AMASA POTTER

In the year 1842 I was moving with my parents from Indiana to Nauvoo, Illinois, and one bright sunny day as we came within three miles of that city we met a buggy with two men in it. The buggy turned out of the road and stopped.

My father was driving our team, and he stopped the horses. The man in the buggy asked if we were moving to Nauvoo. Father replied that we were.

The gentleman in the buggy said, "No doubt you have heard of Joseph Smith the Prophet."

Mother then answered, "We have come five hundred miles to see him."

"I am that man," replied the person in the buggy who acted as spokesman, and then called us all up to the side of the buggy and shook hands with us, and gave Father some instructions about where to go to purchase some land and to settle near the city.

But one thing I remember was, when the Prophet took hold of my hand and said to me, "May God bless you, my little man," I felt a thrill through my whole body like a current of electricity, and I can say that the recollections of my feelings on that occasion have followed me through life, and when dangers on sea and land threatened my destruction,

I have thought of the Prophet Joseph Smith, and all perils have been removed from me.

<small>(Amasa Potter, "A Reminiscence of the Prophet Joseph Smith," *Juvenile Instructor 29*, no. 4 [15 February 1894]: 131–32.)</small>

—•—

ORSON PRATT

In October, 1830, I traveled westward over two hundred miles to see Joseph Smith, the Prophet. I found him in Fayette, Seneca County, New York, residing at the house of Mr. Whitmer. I soon became intimately acquainted with this good man, and also with the witnesses of the Book of Mormon. By my request, on the 4th of November, the Prophet Joseph inquired of the Lord for me, and received the revelation published in the Doctrine and Covenants, (now section 34.)

<small>(Elden J. Watson, comp., *The Orson Pratt Journals* [Salt Lake City: Elden Jay Watson, Publisher, 1975], 9.)</small>

—•—

PARLEY P. PRATT

On our arrival, we found that Brother Joseph Smith, the translator of the Book of Mormon, had returned from Pennsylvania to his father's residence in Manchester, near Palmyra, and there I had the pleasure of seeing him for the first time.

He received me with a hearty welcome, and with that frank and kind manner so universal with him in after years. . . .

President Joseph Smith was in person tall and well built, strong and active; of a light complexion, light hair, blue eyes, very little beard, and of an expression peculiar to himself, on which the eye naturally rested with interest, and was never weary of beholding. His countenance was ever mild, affable, beaming with intelligence and benevolence; mingled with a look of interest and an unconscious smile, or cheerfulness, and entirely free from all restraint or affectation of gravity; and there was something connected with the serene and steady penetrating glance of his eye, as if he would penetrate the deepest abyss of the human heart, gaze into eternity, penetrate the heavens, and comprehend all worlds.

He possessed a noble boldness and independence of character; his manner was easy and familiar; his rebuke terrible as the lion; his benevolence unbounded as the ocean; his intelligence universal, and his language abounding in original eloquence peculiar to himself—not polished—not studied—not smoothed and softened by education and refined by art; but flowing forth in its own native simplicity, and profusely abounding in variety of subject and manner. He interested and edified, while, at the same time, he amused and entertained his audience; and none listened to him that were ever weary with his discourse. I have even known him to retain a congregation of willing and anxious listeners for many hours together, in the midst of cold or sunshine, rain or wind, while they were laughing at one moment and weeping the next. Even his most bitter enemies were generally overcome, if he could once get their ears.

I have known him when chained and surrounded with armed murderers and assassins who were heaping upon him every possible insult and abuse, rise up in the majesty of a son of God and rebuke them, in the name of Jesus Christ, till they quailed before him, dropped their weapons, and, on their knees, begged his pardon, and ceased their abuse.

In short, in him the characters of a Daniel and a Cyrus were wonderfully blended. The gifts, wisdom, and devotion of a Daniel were united with the boldness, courage, temperance, perseverance, and generosity of a Cyrus. And had he been spared a martyr's fate till mature manhood and age, he was certainly endowed with powers and ability to have revolutionized the world in many respects, and to have transmitted to posterity a name associated with more brilliant and glorious acts than has yet fallen to the lot of mortals.

As it is, his works will live to endless ages, an unnumbered millions yet unborn will mention his name with honor, as a noble instrument in the hands of God, who, during his short and youthful career, laid the foundation of that kingdom spoken of by Daniel, the prophet, which should break in pieces all other kingdoms and stand forever.

(*Autobiography of Parley P. Pratt,* [Salt Lake City, Utah: Deseret Book, 1985], 31–32.)

— • —

MR. REED

The first acquaintance I had with General Smith was about the year 1823. He came into my neighborhood, being then about eighteen years of age, and resided there two years, during which time I became intimately acquainted with him. I do know that his character was irreproachable; that he was well known for truth and uprightness; that he moved in the first circles of community, and he was often spoken of as a young man of intelligence, and good morals, and possessing a mind susceptible of the highest intellectual attainments.

(*Times and Seasons,* 1 June 1844, 549.)

— • —

JAMES HENRY ROLLINS

As early as February 1831, I first met Joseph Smith in my Uncle Sidney Gilbert's house. This was the first day he arrived in Kirtland, and while he was in the house conversing with my uncle and aunt, I, being at the front gate, saw a wagon turn over as it was coming down the slippery hill, and heard a woman and two or three children screaming. This was Joseph's family. I ran in and told Joseph and Uncle about it, and Joseph ran to assist them without his hat. My first impression was, that if any of the occupants were hurt seriously that Joseph could heal them, but none of them were hurt.

Joseph and my uncle returned to the house. He asked my uncle if I was his son. He said, "No, I was his wife's nephew," "Well," he said, "the Lord has shown him great things." I truly had seen Joseph and Hyrum in my vision in December 1830.

After the turning over of the wagon Joseph and his wife, Emma, came to my uncle's house for the purpose of finding a house to suit her. Soon after this, more or all of the Smith family arrived in Kirtland. From this time on I became personally acquainted with the Smith family.

("A Life Sketch of James Henry Rollins [1816–1839]," typescript copy, BYU Special Collections, Harold B. Lee Library, Provo, Utah, 2.)

ABRAHAM ROSE

The gospel of the Church of Jesus Christ of Latter-day Saints was brought to the Rose home in 1836 by Apostle Orson Hyde. As a result the family, the parents and five children, left their home in Howard and followed the Saints. They sojourned in Carthage, Ohio, for about four years where Abraham engaged in the manufacture of maple sugar and maple syrup; at this place Alley Stephen was born. When the child was two and one-half years of age, the family was driven from their home in Ohio, and after enduring heart-breaking hardships with the Saints, arrived in Nauvoo, Illinois, in October 1843. On seeing the Prophet Joseph Smith for the first time, they were impressed with his noble appearance. Here Abraham was appointed by the Prophet to be president of one of the Church branches just out of Nauvoo, called the Lima Branch.

("From His Records," in Kate B. Carter, comp. *Our Pioneer Heritage*, 20 vols. [Salt Lake City, Utah: Daughters of the Utah Pioneers, 1958–77], 7:234–35.)

---•---

EDWIN RUSHTON
(RELATED BY HIS SON)

After sailing from England, our immigrant company reached Nauvoo, April 13, 1843. Father was very anxious to find the members of his family already established there, and hurried towards the town in search of them. He had gone only a short distance when he met a man riding a beautiful black horse. The man accosted him, saying, "Hey, Bub, is that a company of Mormons just landed?"

In much surprise, Father answered, "Yes, sir."

"Are you a Mormon?" the stranger continued.

"Yes, sir," Father again answered.

"What do you know about old Joe Smith?" the stranger asked.

"I know that Joseph Smith is a prophet of God," said Father.

"I suppose you are looking for an old man with a long, gray beard. What would you think if I told you I was Joseph Smith?" the man continued.

"If you are Joseph Smith," said Father, "I know you are a prophet of God."

In a gentle voice, the man explained, "I am Joseph Smith. I came to meet the people, dressed as I am in rough clothes and speaking in this manner, to see if their faith is strong enough to stand the things they must meet. If not they should turn back right now."

This was Father's introduction to the Prophet.

(Edwin Rushton, *Pioneer Journals*, 2–3.)

—•—

BATHSHEBA W. SMITH

We went to Illinois in February, 1839, but did not see the Prophet Joseph until the spring, when he got out of prison and came to Illinois. A conference was called soon after Joseph and his brethren arrived at Quincy.

My brother took my sisters and me and went to that conference, and there I saw Joseph for the first time and heard him preach. I knew he was a Prophet of God, when I joined the Church before I saw him; my testimony was strengthened when I heard him preach, though at this time I did not get to speak to him. I do not remember just when I did first speak to him and shake hands with him.

The Prophet was a handsome man—splendid looking, a large man, tall and fair and his hair was light. He had a very nice complexion, his eyes were blue, and his hair a golden brown and very pretty.

(Bathsheba W. Smith, "Joseph Smith, the Prophet," *Young Woman's Journal 16*, no. 12 [December 1905]: 549–50.)

My first impressions were that he was an extraordinary man—a man of great penetration; was different from any other man I ever saw, had the most heavenly countenance; was genial, affable and kind, and looked the soul of honor and integrity.

(*The Juvenile Instructor*, XXVII [1 June 1892]: 344.)

———•———

GEORGE A. SMITH

Friday, May 25 (1833), we arrived at Kirtland, Ohio, having traveled five hundred miles. We found our brethren and sisters all well and very glad to see us. We were heartily welcomed by my cousin Joseph, the Prophet. It was the first time I had seen him. He conducted us to his father, who lived in a large log house.

("Memoirs of George A. Smith," typescript copy, BYU Special Collections, Harold B. Lee Library, Provo, Utah, 9.)

———•———

JESSE N. SMITH

I first saw the Prophet in Kirtland, though I was then but a child. Afterward I met him at Nauvoo. The Prophet was incomparably the most God-like man I ever saw. I know that by nature he was incapable of lying and deceitfulness, possessing the greatest kindness and nobility of character. I felt when in his presence that he could read me through and through. I know he was all that he claimed to be.

(*Juvenile Instructor*, XXVII [1 January 1892]: 23.)

———•———

JOB F. SMITH

Starting about the 5th of March 1843, we set sail on the ship *Yorkshire* from Liverpool for New Orleans, which port was reached in about ten weeks, reaching Nauvoo on the 31st of May following. At the landing we were met by the Prophet Joseph Smith and apostle Brigham Young, both of whom greeted us, the prophet referring us to Brigham for answer to questions they might wish to propound and for such advice as might be found necessary to give the company temporary homes.

(Diary of Job Smith, a Pioneer of Nauvoo, Illinois, and Utah, typescript copy, Huntington Library, San Marino, California, 4–5.)

The first time that I saw him was on the banks of the Mississippi River on the 31st of May 1843. It was the usual landing place, and as a boat could be seen ploughing its way against a stiff current, a considerable crowd including the Prophet and Brigham had gathered to meet a company of expected immigrants.

("My Recollections of the Prophet During the Last Year of His Life, from a Manuscript Written by Job Smith," LDS Church Archives, Salt Lake City, Utah.)

JOSEPH F. SMITH

As a child I . . . listened to him preach the gospel that God had committed to his charge and care. As a child I was familiar in his home, in his household, as I was familiar under my own father's roof. I have retained the witness of the Spirit that I was imbued with as a child and that I received from my mother, the firm belief that Joseph Smith was a prophet of God; that he was inspired as no other man in this generation, or for centuries before had been inspired; that he had been chosen of God to lay the foundations of God's kingdom as well as of God's Church; that by the power of God he was enabled to bring forth the record of the ancient inhabitants of this continent, to revive and reveal to the world the doctrine of Jesus Christ, not only as he taught it in the midst of the Jews in Judea, but as he also taught it, and it was recorded, in greater simplicity and plainness upon this continent, among the descendants of Lehi.

As a child I was impressed deeply with the thought, and firmly with the belief, in my soul that the revelations that had been given to and through Joseph the Prophet, as contained in [the Book of Mormon], the book of Doctrine and Covenants, were the word of God, as were the words of the ancient disciples when they bore record of the Father and the Son."

(Sermon, Salt Lake Assembly Hall, July 8, 1917.)

—•—

LUCY MESERVE SMITH

I was born February 9th, 1817, at Bethel, Oxford County, Maine, and I was baptized August 12th, 1837. I first met the Prophet Joseph Smith on a steamboat, when I landed at the ferry in Nauvoo. The first words he said to our company were: "I guess you are all Latter-day Saints here, by the singing I heard when the boat landed." He then shook hands with each one in the company, and then took his sister, Lucy Millican's seven-month-old boy in his arms and sat down and wept for joy, as his sister was thought to be in a decline when she left home the year before with her husband. She was indeed the picture of health when she returned, which gave the Prophet double joy on meeting her with her son.

President Joseph Smith, the Prophet, looked the same to me when I met him as I saw him in a dream before I left home. I can bear testimony that many of his prophecies have come to pass; not only his alone, but others who have been ordained under his administration, have uttered prophecies that have been fulfilled, to the letter.

(Lucy M. Smith, "Recollections of the Prophet Joseph Smith," *Juvenile Instructor 27*, no. 15 [1 August 1892]: 470.)

— • —

ELIZA R. SNOW

In the autumn of 1829, I heard of Joseph Smith as a prophet to whom the Lord was speaking from the heavens and that a sacred record containing a history of the origin of the aborigines of America was unearthed. A prophet of God, the voice of God revealing to man as in former dispensations—this was what my soul had hungered for. But could it be true? I considered it a hoax—too good to be true.

In the winter of 1830 and 31, Joseph Smith called at my father's home. As he sat warming himself, I scrutinized his face as closely as I could without attracting his, and decided that his was an honest face. My adopted motto, "Prove all things and hold fast to that which is good," prompted me to investigation, as incredulous as I was.

On the 5th of April, 1835, I was baptized by a Mormon Elder.

(Eliza R. Snow, "Life Sketch," handwritten manuscript. Church Historian's Library, Salt Lake City, Utah: *Women's Exponent*, II (1 January 1874), 117.)

— • —

LORENZO SNOW

The first time I saw Joseph Smith I was seventeen years of age. It was in the fall of 1831. He was going to hold a meeting in Hiram, Portage County, Ohio, about four miles from Father's home. Having heard many stories about him, my curiosity was considerably aroused, and I thought I would take advantage of this opportunity to see and hear him.

When we reached there, the people were already assembled in a small bowery. There were about two hundred and fifty people present. The meeting had already commenced, and Joseph Smith was standing in the door of Father Johnson's house looking into the bowery and addressing the people.

I made a critical examination as to his appearance, his dress, his manner as I heard him speak. He was only twenty-five years of age and was not, at that time, what would be called a fluent speaker. His remarks were confined principally to his own experiences, especially the visitation of the angel, giving strong and powerful testimony in regard to these marvelous manifestations. He simply bore his testimony to what the Lord had manifested to him, to the dispensation of the gospel which had been committed to him, and to the authority he possessed.

At first he seemed a little diffident and spoke in rather a low voice. But as he proceeded, he became very strong and powerful and seemed to affect the whole audience with the feeling that he was honest and sincere. It certainly influenced me in this way, and it made impressions upon me that remain until the present day.

As I looked upon him and listened, I thought to myself that a man bearing such a wonderful testimony as he did, and having such a countenance as he possessed, could hardly be a false prophet. He certainly could not have been deceived, it seemed to me. If he was a deceiver, he was deceiving the people knowingly; for when he testified that he had had a conversation with Jesus, the Son of God, and had talked with him personally, as Moses talked with God upon Mount Sinai, and that he had also heard the voice of the Father, he was telling something that he either knew to be false or to be positively true.

When I went to Kirtland some three or four years later, I was on the street with my sister, Eliza, when Joseph Smith came along. He was in a great hurry, and stopped just long enough to be introduced and shake hands. He turned to my sister and said, "Eliza, bring your brother over to the house to dinner."

She was then boarding at his home and teaching his private school. As he left us I watched him just as far as I could see him, then I turned to my sister and said: "Joseph Smith is a remarkable man; I want to get better acquainted with him. Perhaps, after all, there is something more to Joseph Smith and to Mormonism than I ever dreamed of."

Accordingly, the next time I saw the Prophet was at his own house in Kirtland. He sat down at one end of the table and I sat next to him. He seemed to have changed considerably in his appearance since I first saw him at Hiram, four and a half years before. He was free and easy in his conversation with me, making me feel perfectly at home in his presence. In fact, I felt as free with him as if we had been special friends for years.

(LeRoi C. Snow, "How Lorenzo Snow Found God," *Improvement Era* 40, no. 2 [February 1937]: 83.)

EDWARD STEVENSON

I first saw Joseph Smith at Pontiac, Michigan, in 1834, when he visited the Pontiac Branch. The meetings were crowded. The Prophet stood at a table for a pulpit. Before he got through, he was in the midst of the congregation with uplifted hand.

His countenance seemed to assume a heavenly whiteness. He testified with great power concerning the visit of the Father and the Son and the conversation he had with them. Never before did I feel such power. Though only a small percentage of those who saw and heard him accepted the restored gospel, there was not one who dared to dispute it.

Many were heard to say, "Well, if Mormonism is true, it will stand; if not true, it will fall."

A prediction made by the Prophet was literally fulfilled, Joseph said, "If you will obey the gospel with honest hearts, I promise you in the name of the Lord that the gifts as promised by our Savior will follow you, and by this you may prove me to be a true servant of God."

I both saw and heard the gifts follow those who believed and obeyed the gospel.

(Autobiography of Edward Stevenson, typewritten manuscript, Church Historian's Library, Salt Lake City, Utah, 7–9.)

JOSEPH TAYLOR

When I first saw Joseph Smith I believed he was one of God's noblemen; as I grew older I became thoroughly convinced that he was a true prophet of God.

(Joseph Taylor, "Recollections of the Prophet Joseph Smith," *Juvenile Instructor 27*, no. 7 [1 April 1892]: 202–3.)

WILLIAM TAYLOR

My first acquaintance with the Prophet Joseph Smith began in this way. On my nineteenth birthday, when he appeared at my father's house in the woods, accompanied by my brother, John Taylor [afterward President John Taylor], S. Roundy, and J.D. Parker, about the middle of the night, September 2, 1842. How they ever found their way in the dark is a mystery, for I, who was very familiar with the country, could not have come by so circuitous a route even in the daylight.

Late in the night the Prophet had gone to my brother John's house in Nauvoo and said to him: "I want you to go with me to your father's.' "

My brother said: "But I can't go, Brother Joseph; I am sick in bed!"

The Prophet replied: "I'll come in and help you dress, and you'll find no inconvenience from going out."

So Brother John got up, dressed and started out with him, and by the time they reached our home, none of us could tell he had been the least sick.

(*Young Woman's Journal*, XVII [December 1896]: 547.)

JAMES P. TERRY

My first recollection of the Prophet Joseph Smith was in 1842 or '43. I knew him well from that time on until his death, and often heard him preach. He was preaching one Sunday in the grove west of the temple. I was standing or sitting on the framework back of the stand. In his speaking he said: "If I should tell you or the Latter-day Saints what I know, as good a man as old Father C____ sitting here on the stand would want to take my life."

(James P. Terry, "Recollections of the Prophet Joseph Smith," *Juvenile Instructor* 28, no. 10 [15 May 1893]: 331.)

— • —

JOHN H. TIPPETS

We arrived in Kirtland on the 9th of December, 1834, where we rejoiced to see the Prophet Joseph Smith and the Saints. We visited Brother Joseph this morning on the 9th of December. We presented our letters of recommendation. Had a counsel in the evening by candlelight, it being winter season. We were counseled to stay in Kirtland until the spring . . . which we readily accepted.

("John H. Tippets," Mormon Biography File, LDS Church Archives, Salt Lake City, Utah, 2–3.)

— • —

DANIEL TYLER

[My first impression of the Prophet's character] was that he was a meek, humble, sociable, and very affable man, as a citizen, and one of the most intelligent of men, and a great prophet. My subsequent acquaintance with him more than confirmed my most favorable impressions in every particular. He was a great statesman, philosopher, and philanthropist, logician, and last but not least the greatest prophet, seer and revelator that ever lived save Jesus Christ only.

(*The Junvenile Instructor*, XXVIII [1 Feb. 1892]: 93–95.)

— • —

EMMELINE BLANCHE WELLS

Journeying from my home in Massachusetts to Nauvoo, Illinois, with a company of Latter-day Saints, we were joined in Albany by some elders returning from missions in the eastern states. Among them was the late Jacob Gates, who was accompanied by his wife, with whom I became well acquainted en route. Sister Gates talked a great deal about the Prophet Joseph, whom she knew intimately, and when she saw that I was specially interested in him, promised me that she would introduce me to him on our arrival in Nauvoo. She also told me many things concerning his life and mission that I had not known before; and I listened carefully to all the elders' conversation, for they were full of zeal and the spirit of the Latter-day work and of love for the Prophet Joseph.

To me it was a continuous revelation. Although Sister Gates seemed to think it impossible for one so young and inexperienced to realize the greatness and wonderful power of the Prophet Joseph Smith, in time I came to understand the feeling when I tried to explain to others the power he possessed that impressed the people with whom he came in contact.

As we neared our destination in sailing up the Mississippi, the elders . . . were full of enthusiasm at the thought of seeing the Prophet again. But not once in all the conversation did I hear a description of his personal appearance. There were no photographs in those days, and I had not formed any idea of him except of his wonderful power.

I think in looking back upon that time, I must have been in a state of mingled emotions of astonishment and awe, not knowing what I should do or say on my arrival.

At last the boat reached the upper landing, and a crowd of people were coming toward the bank of the river. As we stepped ashore, the crowd advanced, and I could see one person who towered away and above all the others around him; in fact, I did not see distinctly any others. His majestic bearing, so entirely different from anyone I had ever seen (and I had seen many superior men), was more than a surprise. It was as if I beheld a vision; I seemed to be lifted off my feet, to be as it were walking in the air, and paying no heed whatever to those around me.

I made my way through the crowd. Then I saw this man whom I had noticed, because of his lofty appearance, shaking hands with all the people, men, women, and children.

Before I was aware of it, he came to me, and when he took my hand, I was simply electrified—thrilled through and through to the tips of my fingers, and every part of my body, as if some magic elixir had given me new life and vitality.

I am sure that for a few minutes I was not conscious of motion. I think I stood still. I did not want to speak, or be spoken to. I was overwhelmed with indefinable emotion.

Sister Gates came to me and said, "I'll introduce you to the Prophet Joseph now; he is here."

I replied, "I don't want to be introduced to him."

She was astonished and said curtly, "Why, you told me how desirous you were of meeting him."

I answered, "Yes, but I've seen him and he spoke to me."

"But he didn't know who you were!"

I replied, "I know that, but it don't matter." And Sister Gates walked away without another word of explanation. I was, in reality, too full for utterance.

I think had I been formally presented to the Prophet, I should have fallen down at his feet, I was in such a state of ecstacy.

The one thought that filled my soul was, I have seen the Prophet of God, he has taken me by the hand, and this testimony has never left me in all the "perils by the way." It is as vivid today as ever it was. For many years, I felt it too sacred an experience even to mention.

(Emmeline B. Wells, "Joseph Smith, the Prophet," *Young Woman's Journal* 16, no. 12 [December 1905]: 555.)

———•———

ELIZA WESTOVER

In 1841 we left our native home for Nauvoo, arriving there in May, traveling by canal, rail, and steamboat.

The first to greet us on landing were the Prophet Joseph Smith and Brigham Young. After shaking hands and bidding us welcome, Brother Joseph's first question was had we a place to go.

("Eliza Westover to Lewis B. Westover," 16 July 1916, LDS Church Archives, Salt Lake City, Utah.)

———•———

JOEL WILLIAM WHITE

When I was four my parents then went to Kirtland in 1835. While there I remember going to meetings in the Kirtland Temple and there seeing the Prophet Joseph. My first recollection of seeing him was after meeting one day my mother was talking to Sister Smith when the Prophet came up shaking hands with mother and also with me, my mother telling me that was the Prophet.

("Autobiographical Sketch of the Life of Joel William White 1831–1910," LDS Church Archives, Salt Lake City, Utah, 1–2.)

———•———

ELIZABETH ANN WHITNEY

In December, Joseph Smith, with his wife, Emma, and a servant girl, came to Kirtland in a sleigh; they drove up in front of my husband's store. Joseph jumped out and went in; he reached his hand across the counter to my husband, and called him by name. My husband, not thinking it was anyone in whom he was interested, spoke, saying: "I could not call you by name as you have me." He answered, "I am Joseph the Prophet; you have prayed me here, what do you want of me?" My husband brought them directly to our own house; we were more than glad to welcome them and share with them all the comforts and blessings we enjoyed.

I remarked to my husband that this was the fulfillment of the vision we had seen of a cloud as of glory resting upon our house. And during the time they resided with us, and under our roof, were many of the revelations given which are recorded in the book of Doctrine and Covenants.

(Elizabeth Ann Whitney, "A Leaf from an Autobiography," *Woman's Exponent 7*, no. 7 [1 September 1878]: 51.)

HELEN MAR WHITNEY

Among the many pleasing incidents within my recollection was the sight of a large flatboat loaded with English Saints, who were obliged to leave the steamer at Keokuk, in consequence of low water. They were singing the sweet songs of Zion as they came up the river at the close of the day, and landed near the Prophet's house, where stood scores of the Saints; also many outsiders had gathered there, and Joseph too, who welcomed them to Zion.

(Helen Mar Whitney, "Scenes and Incidents in Nauvoo," *Woman's Exponent 11*, no. 12 [15 November 1882]: 90.)

There is another little incident which I had missed jotting down in the right place. It was near the first of June 1843, just previous to my father's starting east, that the Prophet called and invited him to ride with him and William Clayton, his private clerk, as he was going around to give invitations to his friends, to take a pleasure trip with him down to Quincy, in the little Nauvoo boat which, previous to its being purchased, was called Maid of Iowa. I was also invited to go along. As we drove up the river a Steamer was just landing, and a number of strange gentlemen came ashore, who seemed to have quite a curiosity to see the Prophet. He got out, and in his warm and genial way, gave each of them a cordial shake of the hand. As the carriage was about starting away, one of them came up and, after being introduced by President Smith, requested the privilege of riding. After going a few rods the carriage was stopped for him to get out. He wished to have it said that he rode with Joseph Smith, whom they styled the "American Mahomet."

(Helen Mar Whitney, "Scenes and Incidents in Nauvoo," *Woman's Exponent 11*, no. 8 [15 September 1882]: 68.)

—•—

WALTER WILCOX

The occasion was a meeting held in the temple, the first Sabbath after I arrived there. I watched the people come in and when I saw Joseph Smith, I knew that he was the Prophet of God.

(*Collected Discourses*, edited by Brian H. Stuy, 5 vols. [Burbank, California, and Woodland Hills, Utah: B. H. S. Publishing, 1987–92], 5:34–35.)

—•—

MARY ANN STEARNS WINTERS

To me he seemed larger and nobler than any other man, and when he was introduced as "the Prophet," his mission seemed as sure to me as that I could see the sun shine in the heavens, or that Abraham was a man of God, as my mother had taught me from the Bible.

("An Autobiographical Sketch of the Life of the Late Mary Ann Stearns Winters, Daughter of Mary Ann Stearns Pratt," in "Mary Ann Frost Stearns Pratt," *Relief Society Magazine 3*, no. 8 [August 1916]: 428.)

———•———

CATHERINE HASKELL WOODBURY

It was as if I had beheld a vision. I seemed to be lifted off my feet—to be walking on air. Before I was aware of it, he came to me and took my hand. I was simply electrified—thrilled through and through every part of my body. The one thought that filled my soul was, "I have seen the prophet of God!" The power of God rested upon him to such a degree that on many occasions he seemed translated. The glory of his countenance was beyond description. His voice seemed to shake the place on which he stood and to penetrate the inmost soul of his hearers. The people loved him to adoration.

(Zula Rich Cole, "Ashbel, His Wife and Children," in Kate B. Carter, comp., *Our Pioneer Heritage*, 20 vols. [Salt Lake City, Utah: Daughters of the Utah Pioneers, 1958–77], 3:528.)

———•———

WILFORD WOODRUFF

My first introduction to him was rather singular. I saw him out in the field with his brother Hyrum. He had on a very old hat and was engaged shooting at a mark. I was introduced to him, and he invited me home with him.

I accepted the invitation, and I watched him pretty closely to see what I could learn. He remarked, while passing to his house, that this was the first hour he had spent in recreation for a long time.

Shortly after we arrived at his house. He went into an adjoining room and brought out a wolf-skin, and said, "Brother Woodruff, I want you to help me to tan this." So I pulled off my coat, went to work and helped him, and felt honored in so doing.

He was about going up with the brethren to redeem Zion, and he wanted this wolf-skin to put upon his wagon seat, as he had no buffalo robe.

This was my first introduction to the Prophet Joseph Smith, the great Seer of this last dispensation.

I was not there long before I heard him talk about going to Zion, and it did my soul good to hear him speak of many things concerning Zion, the gathering of Israel, and the great Latter-day work; and I felt truly satisfied with what I saw and heard.

I recollect that in the evening after I got there, several of the brethren came in and talked with brother Joseph, and asked what they should do, for they had not means to bear their expenses from there to Missouri. Brother Joseph said, "I am going to have some money soon"; and the next morning he received a letter containing a hundred and fifty dollars, sent to him by Sister Voce, of Boston.

(Journal of Discourses 7:101 [10 January 1858].)

My first introduction to the Prophet, in 1834, was rather singular. He had on a very old hat and was shooting at a mark. He had a pistol in his hand. Said he, "Brother Woodruff, I've been out shooting at the mark. I wanted to see if I could hit anything. Have you any objection to it?"

"Not at all," said I. "There is no law against a man shooting at a mark that I know of."

He invited me into his house. I accepted the invitation, and I watched him pretty closely to learn what I could. He remarked while passing to his house that this was the first hour he had spent in recreation for a long time.

Shortly after we arrived at his house, he went into an adjoining room and brought out a wolf-skin, and said, "Brother Woodruff, I want you to help me tan this." So I pulled off my coat, went to work and helped him, and felt honored in so doing. He was going with the brethren of Zion's camp, and he wanted this wolf-skin to put upon his wagon seat, as he had no buffalo robe.

This was my first acquaintance with the Prophet Joseph. And from that day until the present I never saw a moment when I had any doubt with regard to this work.

(*Millennial Star*, LIII [5 Oct. 1891]: 627–28.)

———•———

MARIAH WOODWARD

It was in 1841 when I was about seventeen years old that I first saw the Prophet Joseph Smith. I had walked from Middle Tennessee, my birthplace, to Nauvoo, which place I intended to make my home.

In company with my guardian, Brother Alfonzo L. Young, I attended Sunday meeting. We both knew the Prophet as soon as we saw him, and when meeting was out went up and shook hands with him. Brother Young was so overcome with joy that he fell upon the Prophet's breast in tears. Brother Joseph put his arms around him and wept with him.

(Mariah J. Woodward, "Joseph Smith, the Prophet," *Young Woman's Journal 17*, no. 12 [December 1906]: 543–44.)

—•—

ANDREW WORKMAN

I first saw the Prophet in May 1842. He was with about a dozen others on the stand in a meeting. I knew him as soon as I saw him. Although I was young I knew him to be a man of God.

A few days after this I was at Joseph's house; he was there, and several men were sitting on the fence. Joseph came out and spoke to us all. Pretty soon a man came up and said that a poor brother who lived out some distance had had his house burned down the night before. Nearly all of the men said they felt sorry for the man. Joseph put his hand in his pocket, took out five dollars and said: "I feel sorry for this man to the amount of five dollars; how much do you all feel sorry?"

(*The Juvenile Instructor*, XXVII [15 October 1892]: 641.)

—•—

BRIGHAM YOUNG

In the fall of 1832, Brothers Heber C. Kimball, Joseph Young, and myself started for Kirtland to see the Prophet Joseph. We went to his father's house and learned that he was chopping wood. We immediately went to the woods, where we found the Prophet and two or three of his brothers. Here my joy was full at the privilege of shaking the hand of the Prophet of God, and I received the sure testimony, by the spirit of prophecy, that he was all that any man could believe him to be, as a true prophet. He was happy to see us, and made us welcome.

In the evening a few of the brethren came in, and we conversed together upon the things of the kingdom. Joseph called upon me to pray. In my prayer I spoke in tongues, which gift I had previously received and excercised. As soon as we arose from our knees, the brethren flocked around him and asked his opinion concerning the gift of tongues that was upon me. He told them that it was the pure Adamic language. Some said to him they expected he would condemn the gift Brother Brigham had, but he said, "No, it is of God, and the time will come when Brother Brigham Young will preside over this Church."

The latter part of this conversation was in my absence.

(*Millennial Star*, XXI [11 July 1863]: 439.)

Douglas J. Vermeeren

Douglas Vermeeren has taught the gospel as a full-time missionary in Belgium, a full-time and early morning Seminary teacher, and a Gospel Principles and Gospel Doctrine teacher.

Doug was a featured speaker at Ricks College's (now BYU—Idaho) Issues and Interactions symposium (speaking on the Garden of Gethsemane) and was Ricks College's first student academic lecturer to speak on the book of Abraham. He has written articles for the *Ensign*, the *New Era*, and the *Friend*.

Doug works as an achievement expert and motivational speaker, talking to hundreds of people each year on how to get to their goals instantly. He was the first North American to ever address the Chinese government leaders on achievement and performance. While in China he developed a program for Chinese university teachers to be more effective instructors of English. For his work with this program the Wu Zhai university awarded him the distinction of Visiting Professor.

Doug and his sweetheart, Holly, live in Calgary, Alberta, Canada. Together they have three children: Julienne, Jordan, and Jared.

You can find out more about Doug on his website, www.DouglasVermeeren.com.